D1175887

★ ★

WAR HEROES OF AMERICA

Paul Revere

PATRIOT AND CRAFTSMAN

MATTHEW G. GRANT

Illustrated by John Keely and Dick Brude

GALLERY OF GREAT AMERICANS SERIES

★ ★

Paul Revere

PATRIOT AND CRAFTSMAN

Text copyright © 1974 by Publication Associates. Illustrations copyright © 1974 by Creative Education. International copyrights reserved in all countries. No part of this book may be reproduced in any form without written permission from the publisher. Printed in the United States.

Library of Congress Number: 73-18076   ISBN: 0-87191-303-8

Published by Creative Education, Mankato, Minnesota 56001

Library of Congress Cataloging in Publication Data
Grant, Matthew G
  Paul Revere — patriot and craftsman.
  (His Gallery of great Americans series. War heroes of America)
  SUMMARY: A brief biography of Paul Revere stressing his patriotic acts and his skill as a silversmith.
  1. Revere, Paul, 1735-1818 — Juvenile literature. (1. Revere, Paul, 1735-1818. 2. United States — History — Revolution — Biography) I. Keely, John, illus. II. Title.
F69.R4215   973.3'311'0924 (B) (92)   73-18076
ISBN 0-87191-303-8

CONTENTS

NORTH BRIDGE

CONCORD

PAUL REVERE

MYSTIC R.

BRITISH ADVANCE

BRITISH RETREAT

BUNKER HILL

CHARLES RIVER

GEORGE WASHINGTON

THE START OF THE WAR

 PAUL REVERE-HEROIC RIDE
BRITISH ADVANCE
BRITISH RETREAT

SILVERSMITH OF BOSTON

Young Paul's father was a silversmith, born in France. He came to America because he wanted religious freedom. His French name, Rivoire, was hard for Americans to say. So he changed it to Revere.

Paul Revere learned his father's trade. It was a quiet sort of job, making rings, spurs, buckles, spoons, and teapots. But Paul was not a quiet boy. He was bold and lively and liked action.

Paul learned to ride on borrowed horses. He earned extra money by ringing bells in Christ Church, now known as the Old North Church. Its steeple was so tall that the bells could be heard all over Boston.

In 1754, when Paul was 18, his father died. Paul was able to take care of his mother and his five sisters and brothers because he was a very good silversmith.

The French and Indian Wars were dragging on in those days. Paul served in the Massachusetts Militia for a few months as an artillery lieutenant. He didn't do much fighting. But his hitch in the militia taught him to dislike

the British army very much.

Paul went home to Boston, got married, and settled down. For awhile, he was prosperous. Then the British government started taxing its American colonies heavily. Paul's business declined because people no longer had money to spare for beautiful silver. The people of Boston grumbled bitterly about British rule.

They had no vote and could not control the way they were governed. Men whispered a forbidden word: "Liberty."

A number of young men—including Paul Revere—joined political clubs and complained about British injustice. Paul even engraved some political cartoons poking fun at England. Boston became a center for rebels who plotted freedom for America. The best-known rebels were John Hancock and Samuel Adams. Paul belonged to their club, the Sons of Liberty. He often carried messages to plotters who lived in other towns.

TROUBLE IN BOSTON

British troops were stationed in Boston. The people hated them and often teased them. In 1770, a riot called the Boston Massacre broke out. The redcoats killed five Boston men.

Paul Revere engraved a famous picture of the Massacre. It was widely sold and helped work the people up against British rule.

In 1773, three ships loaded with British tea came to the city. There was a tax on tea and the Sons of Liberty decided that the tea must be destroyed as a gesture of protest against the King. A mob, dressed like Indians, marched to the harbor.

Paul Revere led one group of "Indians."
They dumped all the tea into the water. As
a punishment for this "Boston Tea Party,"
Boston Harbor was closed by the British.
Business came to a standstill. The city was al-
most an island in those days and most of its
food and supplies came in by boat. If the harbor
was closed for long, the people would starve.

Paul carried this news to New York and
Philadelphia.

PAUL REVERE'S RIDES

The thirteen colonies had never united against Britain. But now they got together for the first time and sent food to the suffering people of Boston. Talk of revolt spread through America.

The First Continental Congress met in Philadelphia in 1774. Paul Revere rode with a message from the people of Massachusetts, asking for support in case of a British attack. The Congress agreed.

Meanwhile, Massachusetts patriots gathered guns and supplies. They called themselves "Minutemen" because they were prepared to go to war at a minute's notice.

The following spring, the British governor, General Gage, decided to smash the rebels. He planned to take his army from Boston to Concord, where the Minutemen had hidden their guns. Paul learned of this. He rode out on Easter Sunday, April 16, 1775, and warned the people of Concord to hide their arms and gunpowder. The trip he made, the "first ride" of Paul Revere, is not nearly so well known as the ride he made two days later.

On April 18, Paul learned that the British army was moving out of Boston. He had two lanterns put into the steeple of Christ Church. This pre-arranged signal was to warn patriots in Charlestown, across a neck of the sea from Boston, that the British were coming by ship.

To make sure the warning was spread, Boston patriots sent out two riders: Billy Dawes and Paul Revere. Dawes left Boston by land. Paul escaped by boat.

Landing in Charlestown, Paul borrowed a horse named Brown Beauty from his friend, Deacon Larkin. Then he galloped off to Lexington, to warn John Hancock and Sam Adams that the British army was coming. General Gage planned to arrest the two leaders and ship them off to England for trial.

As Paul rode toward Lexington, he roused the farmers by shouting, "The British regulars are out!"

Paul found Hancock and Adams and warned them. They then decided that Paul, Billy Dawes, and a man named Samuel Prescott should ride together to alert the Minutemen at Concord. The three started off. But they ran into a British patrol. Paul was captured and Dawes lost his horse. But Prescott got through with the warning.

The British let Paul go a few hours later. He was able to help Hancock and Adams escape.

SOLDIER AND BUSINESSMAN

The British fought the Minutemen at Lexington and Concord. These brief battles signaled the start of the American war for independence. Once again, Paul Revere served as an artillery officer.

He was put in command of a fort in Boston Harbor after the British were driven from the city. As a soldier, he was not much of a success. The one expedition he went on, a 1779 foray into Maine, was a fiasco. Paul had been a great spy and messenger, but his talents did not include military genius.

When the war ended, he returned to the work he knew best: he engraved plates for the first paper money printed in the United States.

But his most important service to the young United States was yet to come. Early in the 1800's, he discovered an important industrial secret—how to roll copper into sheets. These sheets were vital for sheathing the bottoms of warships. If Paul had not discovered the secret of rolling copper, America would not have been able to build a navy—and Britain might have been able to re-conquer its lost colony.

Paul's business was a great success. It exists to this day as Revere Copper and Brass, Inc. The many beautiful pieces of silver that Paul Revere made are still greatly admired and often copied for modern buyers. They are considered true works of art.

Paul Revere died peacefully in 1818 at the age of 83. His midnight ride was immortalized in a poem by Henry Wadsworth Longfellow.

GALLERY OF GREAT AMERICANS SERIES

INDIANS OF AMERICA
GERONIMO
CRAZY HORSE
CHIEF JOSEPH
PONTIAC
SQUANTO
OSCEOLA

EXPLORERS OF AMERICA
COLUMBUS
LEIF ERICSON
DeSOTO
LEWIS AND CLARK
CHAMPLAIN
CORONADO

FRONTIERSMEN OF AMERICA
DANIEL BOONE
BUFFALO BILL
JIM BRIDGER
FRANCIS MARION
DAVY CROCKETT
KIT CARSON

WAR HEROES OF AMERICA
JOHN PAUL JONES
PAUL REVERE
ROBERT E. LEE
ULYSSES S. GRANT
SAM HOUSTON
LAFAYETTE

WOMEN OF AMERICA
CLARA BARTON
JANE ADDAMS
ELIZABETH BLACKWELL
HARRIET TUBMAN
SUSAN B. ANTHONY
DOLLEY MADISON

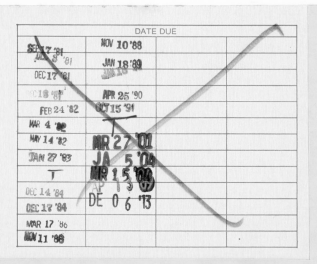